Other Books by Thelma T. Reyna

FICTION:
The Heavens Weep for Us and Other Stories (2009)

POETRY:
Breath & Bone (2011)
Hearts in Common (2013)
Rising, Falling, All of Us (2014)
Reading Tea Leaves After Trump (2018)

AS EDITOR:
Altadena Poetry Review: Anthology 2015
Altadena Poetry Review: Anthology 2016

Dearest Papa

A Memoir in Poems

Thelma T. Reyna

Copyright © 2020 by Thelma T. Reyna

All rights reserved. No part of this book may be used or reproduced in any manner whatsoever, electronic or mechanical—including photocopying, recording, or by any information storage and retrieval system—without written permission by the publisher, except in the case of brief quotations embodied in critical articles and reviews.

Published by Golden Foothills Press
Pasadena, CA 91104
www.GoldenFoothillsPress.com
goldenfoothillspress@yahoo.com

Grateful acknowledgment is made to editors and publishers for permission to reprint poems previously published elsewhere. Credit for prior publication is provided in Acknowledgments section at the end of this book.

ISBN 978-0-578-64373-1

Cover photo: "Bridge in the fog of an early beautiful morning," #51658198
    www.shutterstock.com
Author photo, back cover: Victor Cass
Cover design: Thelma T. Reyna and Dom Gilormini
Book design: Thelma T. Reyna
Interior photo credits: All uncredited photos were taken by author except for those on pages 4 & 10 (photographer unknown).

Printed in the United States of America

First Edition: 2020

ADVANCE PRAISE FOR
Dearest Papa

A book of love and grief that shows how memory is the sharp needle that sews the fabric of our lives together again. As Thelma Reyna writes so beautifully, "This is how we sink, to rise, how brokenness is patched together again."

—**Cassie Premo Steele, Ph.D.**
Author of *Tongues in Trees*
Professor and Writing Coach

Dearest Papa is a solid, humble testament of how each millisecond of life expands into a bigger story that represents all of us. It is a deep, detailed poetic account of love and coupling, as delicate as tender gets. Yet, as haunting and beautifully bold as naked could ever be.

—**Beverly M. Collins**
Author of *Mud in Magic*
Naji Naaman Literary Prize

Thelma T. Reyna has pinned down "lovely" with these beautifully crafted memoir poems. This is a collection of grieving and healing after losing her 'Dear Papa,' her husband, Victor, after fifty years of marriage. They are intimate, personal poems, and when you finish, you'll want to kiss someone you love.

—**Mary Langer Thompson, Ed.D.**
Author of *Poems in Water*
Senior Poet Laureate of California, 2012

Everyone knows or shall know grief. *Dearest Papa* recounts Reyna's passage through her husband's illness, death, absence. She expresses her sorrow through prose poems and verse that create a stunning narrative of minor events unfolding into catastrophe. Readers share the poet's grief, regret, celebration....[and] overwhelming gratitude for life.

—**Michael V. Sedano**,
Co-Founder/Writer/Editor
La Bloga

Thelma Reyna's tribute to her late husband is transcendent. It is a heartfelt look at fifty years of marriage: the misunderstandings, the grief, and through it all, the abiding love. As Reyna writes of the complexities of marriage, "Light and darkness merge, like sun rays piercing storm clouds, opening the sky." This honest account of one woman's journey through grief is a wonder.

—**Judie Rae**
Author of *Howling Down the Moon*
Poet, Novelist, Professional Writing Instructor

Thelma Reyna's *Dearest Papa,* a splendid eulogy to her husband, is composed of delicate poems of scenes from their life together and the meaning of love and caring....a lyrical bouquet of joyful memories and difficult moments of loss.

—**Alejandro Morales, Ph.D.**
Author of *Brick People*
Professor Emeritus, University of California, Irvine

Reyna's latest poetry book, *Dearest Papa,* is more than a widow's grieving testament to her late husband Victor's life. It is an experience, a journey that the reader takes with the author. The book's five-part structure travels in a rising range of emotions, both lows and highs. These tales and poems are unforgettable, and like the subject of loss, universal and yet somehow uplifting. Reyna's recipe for healing includes finding solace in nature.

—**Carolyn Clark, Ph.D.**
Author of *New Found Land*
Professor and Writing Coach

In memory of my husband,
Victor A. Reyna, Jr.--
lovingly called "Papa," first by our three grandchildren,
then by all of us who knew and cherished him.

"Stories do not end."
--Anais Nin

AUTHOR'S FOREWORD

On February 3, 2018, my husband and I celebrated a milestone event, our 50th wedding anniversary. We celebrated it privately, just him and me at our favorite local restaurant, relishing our favorite sushi dishes on a quiet weekday evening. He presented me with a gold chain necklace with intertwined hearts. We ate joyfully and marveled at how far he and I had come in our marriage.

Our wedding in my small, dusty Texas hometown had been inauspicious, a home ceremony with about 30 relatives and friends in attendance. I wore a white, knee-length dress and a short veil that had been handmade the day before by my favorite aunt. My husband wore the only suit he owned. Our best man was my older brother, with his wife the matron of honor. Our matching wedding rings were a simple gold band, which I still wear. At that time, each one cost $25. My mother and a few aunts cooked pots of Spanish rice and beans, made sweet iced tea and Kool-Aid in two large pitchers, and laid out cookies and modest snacks on paper plates at our dining table. The wedding cake was bought at the local supermarket.

I tell you all this with awe at how our lives, all lives, unspool with time, how expected paths take unexpected turns and how the unexpected awaits at each curve in our journeys. Two young Latino college students from backgrounds of poverty, with divergent life stories and roots, made vows to live life together—vows buffeted through five decades, vows challenged as our children were born and our careers unfolded, vows tested as we evolved in our values and perspectives on matters miniscule and mighty. But the most vital of all held constant: our commitment to our little family and one another. No long marriage survives life's vicissitudes without crises, and no long marriage that survives does not evolve into something grander than the spouses.

My husband died suddenly in minor surgery on October 5, eight months after our 50th anniversary. We had plans for an early dinner at our favorite restaurant—the same one described above—after his outpatient procedure. That morning, before I drove us to the hospital, he'd donned a brand-new turquoise shirt and modeled it for me. He beamed as he told me the scale that morning showed he'd met his weight loss goal. We headed out the door, my slimmer, styling husband and I holding hands, not knowing that he'd never walk through that doorway again.

I tell you all this with reverence for what we, all of us, don't know, and with dismay that many of us live every day with unmoored assumptions of our longevity. We clock in and out of interactions with one another, march lockstep in perfunctory duties that we can do, words we can mouth, with dissociation from brain and heart. Not all of us, not all the time. But enough of us, and often enough, that when a loved one is ripped away suddenly, the pain is exponential, epidemic, touching all of us like the ever-spreading concentric circles of an atomic bomb.

Hardly a day passes that I don't think of an incident, a conversation, no matter how trivial, that I had with my husband, particularly in the last two years of his life, when his health was failing, wherein I am not moved by regret at what I said or failed to say to him. I wish the wife back then knew clearly what the widow now knows...about impermanence, about ensuring that our loved ones know clearly and unfailingly how much they mean to us, how much they enrich our lives, because we're telling them regularly, with heart and soul.

In my small book here, I attempt to show how these threads of life are interwoven, with relationships evolving and surviving as love, family, and nature line up to mitigate the stab of loss. It is a modest memoir of my husband's life, and our life together, as well as a tribute to his goodness and devotion. May our dearest Papa be gazing, listening, and smiling his resplendent smile from his other-worldly home.

--Thelma T. Reyna

INTRODUCTION

by Linda Dove, Ph.D.

Thelma Reyna's tender and moving *Dearest Papa* is a love letter to her late husband that serves as a testament to his life but also to hers—for this is a book of elegy, of what's left after loss, in which each word is a powerful act of memorial and yet is never enough.

Reyna has a firm grasp on the elegiac tradition—the repetitions, the obsessions, the questions—but here is also play and whimsy, when she documents Papa's love of gargoyles, or when she recounts how he appoints himself "Champion of the World." She universalizes him in an attempt to make him stay—he is both a stone and a star; he is both embryonic and mummified. There are glimpses into the horror of being left behind, just as there are moments of pure joy at the recognition of what they shared. But mostly—as this is Reyna's book and, thus, her story—there is the effort to continue on despite the overwhelm of grief:

> I walk because I must,
> else lead would spread through rebel bones.
> . . . . . .
> I speak because I must,
> else dust would fill my mouth as his.

In particular, she corrects the record that might serve to erase her own experience, so apparent in her poem addressed to the great Transcendentalist poet, Ralph Waldo Emerson, which begins with an epigraph of his words: "Write it in your heart that every day is the best day of the year." Reyna's poem is defiant in response:

> and though you're always right emerson
> your brain transcending us i must disagree
> emerson for that *one* day that day that one
> day I couldn't save him.

Her syntax breaks down—her proper nouns and pronouns remain uncapitalized, her lines are unpunctuated, her words attempt to lineate the page, spilling over themselves in repetition as she struggles to complete the act of speech. But she can't—her grief takes away the ability to make even the language work.

And, thus, how supercilious and wrongheaded Emerson's commandment appears. How luxurious a thought. In the stark reality of her loss, Reyna's truth transcends his.

With *Dearest Papa*, Reyna has created a poignant and necessary book.

Linda Dove is a Participating Adjunct Professor in the Writing Department of Woodbury University, Los Angeles. She has taught Advanced Composition courses since Fall 2016. In 2017, she started teaching the online publication course and helped birth the University's first national literary magazine, MORIA, staffed by undergraduate student-editors. Dr. Dove is the author of four poetry books and served as Poet Laureate of the Altadena (CA) Library District in 2012-2014.

TABLE OF CONTENTS

1
BEGINNINGS

High School Photo, *3*

Unremembered, *5*

Questions, *6*

Wedding Photo, *9*

Hands Holding Firm, *11*

Spoons, *12*

Gargoyles, *13*

Pete and Tillie, *15*

Stargazers, *16*

Timeless Teaching, *17*

Muscle Envy, *19*

Tools, Tools, *20*

Falling Off Our Roof, *21*

Champion of the World, *23*

The Dog, the Cat, and You, *25*

11.
ENDINGS

Convalescent Hospital, *31*

Cat Bite, *33*

Brave, *36*

Before They Took You Away, *38*

This Is How Grief Goes, *39*

Dear Doctor, *40*

Moment, *41*

Come Say Goodbye, *43*

Like a Politician, No Tears, *45*

Aluminum Sky, *46*

How Poems Are Born, *47*

Named Star, *48*

The Afterward, *49*

Sleepless, *50*

Best Day of the Year, *51*

Come to My Patio, *52*

First Grandchild, *53*

III.
MOURNINGS

Three Bottles, *57*

Potty Cat, *59*

Broken Heart Syndrome, *60*

Our House, *61*

February 3, 2019, *62*

When the Time Comes, *63*

Instead, *64*

Table for One, *66*

Clocks, *67*

Ordinary Things: Tanka Sequence, *68*

Sometimes, *72*

Old Habits, *73*

Dream #1, *74*

Dream #2, *75*

Dream #3, *76*

Lips, Lips, *77*

IV.
BALMS

So Much Goodness in This World, *81*

Cloud Gods, *82*

Trembling Leaf, *83*

Balms, *84*

Bonsai, *86*

Lovely Things, *88*

Stone Hearts, *91*

Birds, Butterflies, and Bees, *92*

V.
RESOLUTIONS

40 Days of Wandering, *95*

Candle, *97*

365 Days, *98*

Piecing the Breakage, *100*

All Our Exploring, *101*

Oak Behind the Dentist's Office, Lake Avenue, *102*

Let There Be Light, *103*

After the Last Act, *104*

Dearest Papa, *105*

❧

Afterword: From a Student, *107*

Acknowledgments, *109*

About Victor A. Reyna, Jr., *111*

About the Author, *115*

1.
Beginnings

HIGH SCHOOL PHOTO

At 17, your life was far away from mine, your posed face slim, lips rounded smooth, slightly tilted head of robust hair pompadoured with modest constraint, not like Rudolf Valentino's, or French kings' wigs. Your hair was the well-oiled hairdo of working-class Latinos. But in this photo, you're the All-American boy, star athlete, a boy I could've had a crush on if I'd known you in your world almost 200 miles away.

Your gaze into the camera is pensive, almost wary but mildly curious, as if measuring the photographer's skill, or waiting for him to call out for the next in line, so you can get on with your day. You, the senior who embraced trigonometry and adored calculus. This is the gaze, the confident, knowing gaze, sitting for your turn in front of the lens, then taking this tilt of your handsome head back to school halls, to friends, labs, lunch, football practice, confident on the edge of manhood. This is the self-assured gaze—head cocked, lips half-smiling, eyes earnest—that I would know 200 miles away a half-dozen years later as you trod a different path.

Your half-brother Gerard brought me this photo when he came to your funeral. I'd never seen it, though I'd heard your stories of Brackenridge High in San Antonio, those times of your athletic glory on the field, loyal entourage of pals, college plans with life's doors opening like pages of beloved books. I wish I'd known you then, but I know you now.

I kiss your photo and pin it back on the small bulletin board by my desk.

eternally young
radiance from your past lighting
my mournful days now

oh, if I could touch
and kiss your red striped shirt...
and caress your face

two pasts, two lives, two
young hearts pulsing miles apart...
bound by an image

UNREMEMBERED

"Whatever may be the tensions and the stresses of a particular day, there is always...the trailing beauty of forgotten joy or unremembered peace."
--Howard Thurman*

Little pictures are the dearest— *little,* not in size but in scope or duration, like

the time you crawled through a playground log because our grandgirl Lizzie begged you to, and

you got stuck, but she helped pull your burly body out, so all was laughter and delight. Decades

prior, long before our wedding, our children, our college graduation, you borrowed

a roommate's car to drive across town at night, with a platter of rice and chicken you'd made and

covered with foil, to take to me at the library, because you knew I'd be hungry, broke, studying late and

hadn't eaten all day and had no ride home, across town. Just a little thing making all the difference in the world.

---

*Quoted by Ava Du Vernay, in "From the Editor." Guest Poet, *TIME* Magazine, February 18-25, 2019

QUESTIONS

For my husband: Take all the time you need. You have eternity. Just get back to me.

∞

Round One:

Did your mother hug you close before she ghosted you, though you were barely two? Did she weep or put on bravado like lipstick?

Did your mother confess you were her pharaoh's treasure, the most blinding, glorious sun, the most precious star in her galaxy?

Did she set you gently—you in your little sailor suit, white cap cocked so cutely—in your neighbor's arms without looking back as she scurried away?

Did your heart feel bitten in half, the wound a pit not known before? Or did the balm of babyhood smother pains unformed, unnamed?

Did you call out when feeding time swung 'round and your mother's hands were gone? Did you toddle out the neighbor's door and seek her face?

Did your father yell and throw his cup against the wall when he found out after work? Did he scoop you in his arms and promise that you'd never, ever be alone?

∞
Round Two:

Did you dream of her when years unspooled, you a virtual orphan scuttled to boarding schools? Did priests and wooden rulers on knuckles help you forget?

Did your father tell you why she left and where? Did he count on miles and months to erase her face as you grew to puberty and wondered why women cry?

Did you feel alone when mothers filled school halls with doting smiles and hugged their boys' diplomas to their breasts? Did you scan the audience for your dad?

Did the rains sing sad when you lived alone, far from home, your high school years? Did jocks and locker room talk and books towering by bed help make you a man?

∞
Round Three:

Did you dream of a princess with a college degree, a beauty queen smart and tall? Did you walk the halls, head high, heart trembling with hope and doubt?

Did you see me at the back of class one criss-crossed day, stacked books on my desk, face still as students filed in? Did your gaze swing quickly past?

Did you see something of merit in me, solitary and plain? Did your soul look deeper than queens, princesses, beauty, and the odds of beating the odds?

Did you see decades unfolding in dissimilar paths, decades of growing, of toiling, creating new stories to move us ahead? Did you never lose hope?

WEDDING PHOTO

The Polaroid is small, dimly lit, clearly not the work of hired hands. The four of us--two men, two women pale as their garb—split the frame in two. The left side is dark, the suits of groom and best man black and smooth, one blending with the other in the gloom, shoulders touching, blurring. The groom tilts his head forward, smiling, eager for the ceremony to commence. The best man, my older brother Roy, an Army man, is squinting, as if trying to see through dusk, entering a zone, trying to decipher contours of the road ahead.

The right side of the photo is suffused in light. Our matron of honor, my brother's wife, and I wear sleeveless dresses, both modest, high-necked, off-the-rack from Penney's. Our fair-skinned arms touch and match, as the men's suited arms became one. Her pale face and mine align side to side, both reposed, our 60's hairdos flipping on our shoulders, bangs brushed across foreheads. All four of us are young, in our 20's, on the cusp of life's treachery, or life's bounty, but on the cusp, and our hearts tremble in unison with uncertainty, with anxieties and dreams, with more gumption than assuredness, but betting on love.

We took the lead—new generation that we were—in being in the spotlight here, carrying commitment forward, as our ancestors did, embracing fragile faith that we'd all prevail.

Light and darkness merge,
like sun rays piercing storm clouds,
opening the sky.

Bunched together, all
shoulders touching side to side,
hearts and bodies one.

Vows are told with hands
held firm, eyes clear, hearts pulsing,
inseparable.

HANDS HOLDING FIRM

If hands could laugh, ours would've pealed our way
   through Rome's catacombs, Spanish Steps, thousand cats
     lounging in Coliseum ruins,

and everywhere we roamed on every wheel that
   turned—buses, taxis, trains—hands holding firm to
     one another, vacationers in love, when we were

young, languoring with afternoon hands circling
   warm on weary flesh, sun gilding balconies
     outside french doors and marble floors in

alabaster rooms built centuries ago, where
   foreign hands speak sentences and poems in
     flourishes, and icon cities are for

lovers with palms clasped whenever we strolled
   cobblestones, our paths just one, one direction,
     together regardless of where.

SPOONS

"Just now, a moment from years ago:
the early morning light, the deft, sweet
gesture of your hand..."
--Mary Oliver*

You gathered me into a fetus in your arms
       and we lay front to back
              like spoons
          in sleepless embryo hours
   front to back
                like spoons

   I fit myself against your throb
your brown arms shielding
                  my lilting pulse
        crisscrossing my breasts to fuse
       my heat with yours

Your muscled thighs pushed mine
      your lips open like a nursing babe's
         trailed silver on my nape
I pushed harder against you
                like spoons

---

*"Quotation is from Mary Oliver's poem, "I Don't Want to Lose," in *Felicity*.

GARGOYLES

these stone miscreants populated your bookshelves till I moved them out to paint

they frown, scowl, bare teeth in teams now on the patio racks

this one, arms entwined on chest, daring me to touch anything he guards

this one, legs crossed, face in book, still menaces with claws dragging by his knees

that one by the pencil cactus crouches on a castle roof to keep out crooks

twelve of them, not lined like suspects in a crime, but parked like guards at swank events

medieval spirits quaked at their batlike wings,
scaly legs and arms

didn't dare step in a courtyard shadowed by these demons on the side of right

you loved these, sought them out at antique stores and fairs, brought them home with pride

you saw their worth, these ugly beings, knew that appearances aren't everything.

PETE AND TILLIE

When my breasts were young and round, my husband named them one night as we lay in afterward euphoria.

Pete.
and.
Tillie.

He tapped each one with a fingertip light as a feather's tip. Monarch knighting heroes with the delicate touch of a sword. Pete and Tillie.

Sounded like a Texas saloon, or a rock band (country?), or a law firm, or a boutique in West LA. Two dogs in a neighbor's house? Could've been all these, but no.

These were my skin, my veins, my capillaries, small outcroppings on the landscape of my flesh filling with blood, flushing, when his fingers alighted.

Women's boobs, docs say, are almost always asymmetric. *Pete's the bigger one,* my husband murmured as his fingers gently traced my right breast. *And Tillie's more feminine, slightly smaller,* he said in scientific tones.

His lips brushed each one gently, back and forth that night, wanting neither boob to feel ignored. *Now you, Pete. Now you, Tillie.* Back and forth, back and forth, his eyes closed, his lips smiling when he rolled onto his back and said again, *Pete and Tillie,* and sighed for his job well done.

STARGAZERS

in the evening, after dinner,
you'd take a blanket and our two kids
to the hood of our car

in the driveway, help them
clamber to the warmth and lean
against the windshield, you

bookended between both,
all with legs extended, faces pasted
to celestial darkness

and tiny shards of stars
that you identified to them,
your arm extended like

a pointer, their mesmerized eyes
following your finger picking out
constellations--

naming names, swooping your
arm from Little Dipper to Big,
from Venus and Calliope to

the Bear, the Archer, the
Milky Way, Orion's Belt, and
explaining "light years" in primary

school terms, chatting about
spaceships and suits, about planets
spinning 'round the sun, our

earth a large blue marble,
with the math teacher turned
astrophysicist unfurling to his

precious children the infinite
grace and luminescence
of heaven

TIMELESS TEACHING

*"Blessed is the influence of one true, loving
human soul on another."
--George Eliot*

My husband never let clocks dictate his caring for his high school students, who looked to him for help in solving problems as immensely diverse as they themselves were—problems of the heart, problems beyond books, beyond calculus or trig. One student, an ethnic-minority child from a disadvantaged home, played on Vic's tennis team. This young man, Paul, was buffeted by family imbroglios, skipped classes, and was on the brink of expulsion from school. Vic defended Paul at an administrative hearing, advocating for him to be retained and allowed to play sports while he got back on track with academic obligations. Under Vic's stewardship, Paul flourished on the tennis team, which won a major championship that year, and he was one of its stars. Paul is now a successful, renowned school principal and a community leader.

*shrinking flower by
thorny road blossoms with sun,
water, watchful sky*

*children: imperfect
till love's hand extends to them
on each learning path*

*open eyes see heart's
hidden nature, coax it to
noble fruition*

Historic league championship tennis trophy won by coach Papa and his team, 1980

MUSCLE ENVY

You were always muscular,
   not tall, but bound with
      Schwarzenegger thighs and calves.
If high school coaches got medals
        for the bulk of their legs,
          you'd win in a blink.

Your teams' athletes slinked
  behind you to the gym
    to uncover your secret.
Magic powders, steroids?
      A thousand squats?
         Or Rose Bowl hills all week?

In spring and summer, you wore
  shorts to work most days
    for team practice after school.
Made it easy for muscle-envy
      kids to shadow you on campus,
        ogling the size of your thighs.

At Gold's Gym one night
  a weightlifter asked about
    your "blowout workouts."
You see, he trained each day
      for years, he said, yet his
        calves were little brothers to yours.

Your muscles were, as they say,
  "a legend in your own time"—
    "Latino Atlas" crafted with genes.
But once, you chuckled and said,
      "Must be the rice and beans,"
        and flexed your legs for emphasis.

TOOLS, TOOLS

Never knew why you collected tools like
gold, ultimately building a vault, an altar
to them of plywood and pegboards we

shingled and birthed—you master, me
apprentice—an 8x8x8 replete with door and
concrete floor 40 years ago, for

small tools like plumbs, or sledgehammers
Thor would struggle to lift. Always wondered how
you knew so much of tools, why you adored

chests, boxes overflowing like pharaohs' bounty
for the afterlife, crammed into a tomb, a
small room of treasures like our shed. You

taught me all their names, these tools you
wielded like weapons against decline,
or like wands for beautifying

our world, to repair, adorn, create. At your side,
I learned their talents, these tools, your friends:
Phillips screwdriver, crescent wrench, lug wrench,

tack hammer, claw hammer, C clamp, T square,
jig saw, reciprocating saw, awl... yes,
awl as in "all"—

I learned them all, handed them like a
surgeon's nurse to you, used them all, marveled
at all you built...all you taught.

FALLING OFF OUR ROOF

∞

It was almost the end of you 14 years ago, recent retiree unafraid of ladders, summoned by roof shingles frayed and dangling by a nail or two. Alone at home, me at work, you clambered up the aluminum rungs to the roof's edge, a simple feat you'd done before, when your bones were young and muscles strong.

But with your body halfway on shingles, your instincts flared, limbs trembling with alarm, and you knew you couldn't stay aloft. *You will fall!* the ladder yelled, your balance off by smidgens. Your ladder teetered on its toes then took a dive that crashed your body on the concrete walk, your burly weight landing with a monstrous thud, your head missing garden boulders by inches.

Ladders must have gods inside. Yes, ladders must have gods folded in their rungs, must have human sensibilities unknown to us, activated by disaster. Had the ladder lurched a foot more to the side, your head would not survive, so ladder gods made sure they tumbled your body on cement instead and saved your life.

∞

Falling was almost the end of you 14 years ago, as it was almost the end of us who loved you when you languished for weeks in the ICU, kidneys failing, shoulder muscles torn, lungs assailed, hips displaced. But your spirit never flagged, your face glad each day to see nurses flitting in and out, ministering to you, your family at your side, day or night, night and day, clocks irrelevant as your body struggled to right itself again.

Some days you floated in mists, disembodied, deluded, dark, light, afire with fever, alight with pain. But you brought yourself back to the battle, stalwart soul you always were, willing your organs to mend their rends, willing your limbs to be strong.

∞

One day, tubes in arms, as you counted ceiling tiles again, you softly told me about her:

When you fell, body inert with concussion of flesh hitting stone, you alone, conscious, and afraid, a nurse dressed wholly in white—stockings, cap, and all--was walking by and came swiftly to your side. She held your hand, you said, spoke soothingly, reassuring you she wouldn't leave you till help came. Neither of you had a phone, but paramedics were soon on the scene, rushed to your aid, and she walked away. You'd never seen her before in our neighborhood and never saw her again. Your eyes welled when you told me this, days after the fall.

∞

Falling was almost the end of you, dear Papa, 14 years ago. Till your last day on earth, your body bore the wounds: an arm that couldn't rise above your neck, a shoulder stooped, a wobbly gait, kidneys racked. Falling off our fickle roof almost took you, but the fickle ladder aligned itself, last second, with help from its gods, to save your life. And an angel dressed as a nurse kept you awake, consoled your soul, and you survived.

Years later, when I said all this, holding your hand as we sat beneath the gingko tree, our knees touching, your eyes welled.

CHAMPION OF THE WORLD

So random, you declaring yourself "Champion of the World" as we—
two grandkids, you and I—rode

across California Avenue to the ice cream place, and the debate
began, rollicking, fierce, with our grandkids

in the back barely containing themselves in their seat
belts, laughing hard as they demanded

proof from you: *How can you be champion of the whole, wide, entire
planet, Papa?* Indeed,

how could you be? Like little lawyers, Charlie and Cassie laid out fact
after fact why there's no such prize, and how

you just can't be this *champion thing!* I had the front-seat view of
you, your mischief profile, your ersatz-smug

smile as you drove, chin high, insisting to our two angels that you
were *THE Champ!* Your reasons were a riot to

them, and we three wondered why our Papa had gotten
this hare-brained scheme. Looking back now, I see

the eternal, twinkling child-soul in you basking in our laughter on an
ordinary run to the ice cream place.

A thrift store trophy labeled by the grandchildren and given with chuckles and smiles to Papa after the ice-cream-run.

THE DOG, THE CAT, AND YOU

1.

Could've been just two of us,
comfy retirees
coming, going, lounging
without critter hair
on clothes, without
having to kick
the furred ones
off sofas and beds.

But Mollie—the rescue
mutt you got
when she was smaller
than our cat, the new
woman in your life who
commandeered your arms
and lap, who curled
between us
in bed each night,

hogging you and my side—
grew too fast,
got kicked out to her
doggie bed, then trained
you to chauffeur her
daily to the dog park
like a good master.

2.

Mollie and Opie never left your side,
brown fur, gray fur
trailing them each
place they flopped. The last
two years, they saw
much less of you and me,
though it was you
they missed.

Mollie perched on pillows
by the window,
watched with big-eyed envy
as I drove us
out the driveway,
watched tight-lipped
(I believe)
as hours passed and we
weren't home.

When we returned
in purpling hours—
IV treatments done,
bandages rewound—
Mollie clicked claws on the floor,
tap-dancing, her tail wagging
like Texas windmills.

3.

The dog, the cat, and you,
taking walks, taking naps,
cronies stealing snacks,
making McDonalds runs
behind my back,
relishing
unhurried
minutes,
taking
days
one
at
a
time.

11.
Endings

CONVALESCENT HOSPITAL

You were in the convalescent, fourth month, the only
smiling face amongst four patients lined like bowling pins
in skinny metal beds, pinned like pins in cotton coverlets,
contained, wood visages facing swinging door that
swooshed and closed for trays, needles, pills, gauze, and
 all that kept your fellows' faces glum, eyes glazed.

Yesterday you slipped from bed, landed on linoleum dust,
so now they've placed a gel pad at the edge where
slippers hit when you pull yourself upright with knuckles
curled on your walker. Now they watch like hawks, the
star of the alley now, your name in black sharpie
scrawled on caution signs pinned to your bed and walls.

You're always the star: shoulders slooped, buttocks slack,
arm drooping when you sit, glasses smudged with butter
from breakfast biscuits but who cares. Halogen examination
lamps don't out-watt your hopeful eyes. Weary fingers take
your pulse, turn you this way, that, change soiled gowns,
but can't dim the stars that illuminate your smile.

Three dessicated men lined like wood beside you, dozing,
headphones blurring snores, eyes nailed to Fox or HBO,
eyes divorced from wives, sisters, brothers who ceased
pilgrimage to these bedsides months ago. But you, you're
the star unswallowed by black holes, the star unblocked
by eclipses part or whole, starlight blooming undeterred.

CAT BITE

1.

It was just a nip, our Opie's rice-grain teeth putting a pinhead dot on the instep of your right foot, barefoot as you were when you walked across our bathroom floor.

He was, as usual, curled in a comma in your path, little gray fur ball in the way, and your foot gently moved his languid body to the side.

And he struck!
The cat's poison only took two weeks to take a toll.
Your angry foot swelled with a fattened band across your arch, the pinprick dot now twice as large.

Your doctor clucked at you for walking shoeless in your home, scowled at you for keeping mum.

2.

The classic poem comes back to haunt: "For want of a nail, a horseshoe was lost; for want of a horseshoe, a horse was lost...." and on and on, how loss piles high and quick and brings defeat.

Papa, oh Papa! The horse, then soldier, battle, war, and so on, unforeseen loss burgeoning from trivialities.

And so the pinprick, the poison, the redness, the...the...

3.

When gangrene from the bite spread past your arch, past your toe, then two or three, then marched like black ash up your calf...

Surgeons scrambled to contain.
Doctors shook their heads and muttered, *knee, leg.*

They tied you to tubes hanging like acrylic spiders from your arms,
potent drugs flooding your system twice daily,
doctors watching as the leg swelled and threatened to abscond.

4.

For want of a nail...a war was lost.

They sliced your right leg open from crotch to bottom of your foot,
railroad-track stitches glowering like a bloated tattoo along its length.

They cut a vein from your thigh, hooked it to your lower leg, a
roadway for anti-gangrene drugs to flood your calf and stave the rot.

5.

Opie curled in his white Sherpa-wool bed each night,
oblivious to hospitals, IVs, ICUs, and the whole alphabet.
Cats don't worry about spelling or school.
Cats don't care about calendars or cures.
But perhaps Opie wondered why Papa wasn't home.

6.

For want of a nail, a kingdom was lost.

Papa, oh Papa! Three toes pruned like dead stems,
a third of your foot carved out and tossed,
and the Frankenstein zipper disfiguring your leg.

An innocuous nip
from our beloved cat
in the sanctity of our home
wreaked havoc for weeks, then months...

7.

But your leg, sans full foot,
survived, and you limped
along, bandages wrapped
tight and high, foot a short mummy,
you leaning on your walker, at
night, in day, moving
forward—tentative, stoic—forward,
the only path.

BRAVE

I'm not brave like him. When gangrene invaded his flesh and doctors warned him he'd lose his leg, Papa never moaned, groaned, or complained. Never wondered, *Why me?*

They butchered his foot, slicing, scooping decayed bone, leaving his foot's innards open like an abbatoir. They then entwined his foot white. As healing puttered forward, month after month, bacteria crept in behind his heart, virus invaded his lungs, kidneys turned traitors and started shutting down.

But through it all, Papa's eyes shone with gratefulness for each sunset he saw casting its lavender beams through his hospital windows. Papa's spirit stayed stout.

☙

through enervating
pain, stout spirit soldiers on
   like a samurai

                                 days not dark but light
                                making nurses laugh, smile,
                                 keeping morale strong

frail in muscle and bones;
        willpower of steel—
                hero still standing

BEFORE THEY TOOK YOU AWAY

they should've scheduled you early morning
                              as they always did
should've made you fast 6 hours instead of
                              20
should've remembered diabetics die
                              when sugar's low
should've made you first that day
                              not last
should've seen the passing hours weaken you
                              with hunger, thirst
should've remembered this surgery
                              was not urgent
should've said *put on your shirt and shoes*
                              you're going home
                              we've made you wait too long

OR. . .
should've given you just one anesthetic drug
                              not two

. . . should've said put on your shirt and shoes
                              you're going home
                              we've made you wait too long

THIS IS HOW GRIEF GOES

"When we are grieving, people may wonder about us,
and we may wonder about ourselves."
--Elisabeth Kubler-Ross*

When loss is swift, when it strikes like a viper in a pot,
blunting hopes and well-laid plans, the hole
that swallows us is bottomless and fierce.

Emptiness unspools like mummy's tape, endless, frayed, muffling,
gagging, dooming lips and eyes to tombs devoid of words and light,
stripped of loving hands,
caverns of ululations.

Loss flattens us.
But this is how grief goes.
This is how we sink, to rise,
how brokenness is patched together again,
how despair ultimately defies death.

---

*Quotation from book by Kubler-Ross and David Kessler, *On Grief and Grieving: Finding the Meaning of Grief Through the Five Stages of Loss*.
Poem originally appeared in a prior version in the author's book, *Reading Tea Leaves After Trump*.

DEAR DOCTOR

All of us are fallible. You should have offered me a chair when
your scrub nurse summoned me from the waiting
room. Mask pulled around your neck, you should have stood
when I entered, knowing as you did.

You should have spoken soft, looked me in the eye, said
you're moving heaven and earth to save him. You should
have held my hand because you remembered you never
saw him without me.

But all of us are fallible. You sat, I stood, while
your pursed lips played your line *not looking good*
five times. Your warmest lines. As if any other
surgery, you said to me, *return outside and wait.*

You should have known he cupped his life into your
hands before your anesthesia sealed his eyes and stomped
his heart. You should have said *I'm sorry so so very sorry*
before you rose and walked away from me.

MOMENT *

They say you know. Heart or brain or both are still, and your life's been scrubbed offline. Stripped, erased, gone blank. You've been unplugged, pulled back from calendars and clocks.

But scientists say humans know the moment they expire.

How did you feel, my love, when your heart screeched to a halt, one second to the next, stopped on a dime, as soon as anesthesia emptied in your veins? Just minor surgery, we'd been told. Just a little nick in the arm to implant this little device, we'd been told before they wheeled you into that room. But your heart went dead. Did you see the doctor's eyes glued to the screen, line flat and straight, humming not beeping? Did you see your surgeon toss his scalpel on the tray after slicing just a nick, hear him gasping, eyes wide?

They say humans know the moment they expire. They don't fully die for, perhaps, another hour.

Did you see their paddles shocking you, the tube they shoved into your throat, scrambling like bumblebees to start you up again? Did you see them press their palms upon your breast, pushing, pumping, sweating, taking turns and knowing you might be gone? What did they say? Which doctor ran the show? Did anyone exclaim, "Oh no! Oh no!" because it all happened at lightning speed?

They say humans know the moment they expire. They say the brain is still aware.

Did you hear your surgeon say, "I've got to tell his wife." Did you see him pull his face mask off, and did he scurry out the door, a frightened ant? They said compressions on your silent chest went on and on, that your heartbeat blipped back for a tiny flash, then disappeared, fading faster each time. Did you see them staring at the screen, and did anybody cry?

They say humans know the moment they expire.

Did you know I stood outside your room, behind the crowd, when they took me to your ICU? Did you see me standing tiptoed, face like stone, lips trembling as the medical team took turns climbing on a padded stool to press your chest nonstop? Did you see my praying lips, my stoic face awash in fear and hope, though doctors, nurses, medics, techs tired and slowed and shuffled limp-armed out your room?

They say humans know the moment they expire.

How did you feel, my love, to know you left without goodbyes, without a clue you'd not return to us? Did you see me press my face to the tall glass of the darkened wall outside your ICU, not bearing the sight of nurses removing blood and bandages, wiping your still body so I could come into the room to be alone with you?

They say humans know the moment they expire.

Did you see me climb into your bed once nurses left, and did you feel my arms tight across your chest and feel the wetness on your breast? Did you hear me telling you my grief, feel my fingers tracing tubes still bandaged to your arm, the arm they barely cut before your heart sank swiftly into silence? Did you feel my lips on yours?

So much to see, so much to hear when your moment of departure hits. Our loved ones who rushed over when I phoned, each of us hanging on to one another in disbelief. The nurse who brought us water and napkins and fruit to spell us through. Our chairs scraping the floor as we circled your bed and reached out to touch your hands and face, as if we could will you back to life.

Inspired by an article "Scientists Find That Humans Actually Know When They Have Died." Based on research by Dr. Sam Parnia. In braincharm.com/2018/11/27/

COME SAY GOODBYE

I.

The rich and famous never beg for farewells.
When Jackie Kennedy sent word her time was done, gentry filed in fealty for days through her sumptuous rooms, took private turns at her bedside to murmur recollections fond, and tied her last hours neatly in a bow.

When Morrie told Mitch *come on over if you want to say goodbye*, the protégé sped to the famed professor's home and held his twiglet hand as he fought spartan for final breaths.

When Elisabeth K-Ross penned the closing chapter of her book, she said to David *I'm finished* and summoned him to her home soon afterward with a single telephoned word: *Come*.

Miles are never barriers to goodbyes when the renowned issue clarion calls to come. Mountains, rivers, calendars crammed pose no obstacle to the faithful who'll trek like pilgrims to hear whispered words and bear witness to the end.

Come. Come say farewell to me if you care. Soothe my dying heart and rub your salve on bones almost turned to dust, on lungs crumpling like tissue. Look into my eyes and press your ear to my lips, if you care.

The highest of the high are peons when the clock ticks down. Waiting in death's gate, they want to exit life with hands in palms of those they loved. No one wants to die alone, wordless, a terminus unmarked.

II.

My dearest Papa, your most-loved aunt beckoned you from a thousand miles away, decades past, in simple words: *You'll never see me alive again unless you come.* But you couldn't, so you didn't, and never knew if she forgave you.

The day they tucked her in the earth, it drowned your heart that you failed to show, to hold her pale hand and tell her how she sweetened your life with tales of your mother's devotion, how your unknown mother's spirit split in two when she abandoned you, but how your mother...and your aunt...loved you without bounds.

III.

For you, they came from a thousand miles hence, three states and here: students grown to grandparents, a brother, my kin from our first days, fellow classroom warriors, coaches, friends of friends, my friends who'd seen you rapt at our poetic readings and knew a compatriot when they saw one.

But not all, not all who mattered in your life, not all when I sent out the call to come bid farewell. Like your beloved aunt, the disembodied you most likely understood that some might make the trek, some not.

Like your beloved aunt, the disembodied you knew celebrities must fill cathedrals or arenas when they lie in state, must leave this earth with astral shows of adoration to cement their fame.

The rest of us savor our small spheres of friendship or acclaim, and know that unseen, distant grief at our departure does not diminish love in any dose.

LIKE A POLITICIAN, NO TEARS

...my friend told me when the memorial ended, with a sidewise glance at my face as I stepped on clods and burrs on the narrow cemetery path wending my way to my husband's open grave. "It was amazing," he blurted. "In your entire speech, not one tear. Like a politician!"

But yes there were tears. I smiled through them and he was fooled. I spoke softly to solemn faces and there were tears. I recounted my husband's pain and there were tears. My friend, too far back, was fooled by calm.

For three days when my husband died, I cried ducts dry, endured stone throat that swallowed speech. Paths of sun and moon entwined till light and dark.

The paper of my speech was mottled and edges curled with wetness.

blank face, lips moving
--for they must, they must say words—
heart beating limply

broken hearts dissolve
the same in rain or sunbeams
...quiet, loud, unparsed

ALUMINUM SKY

cold sheet taut above trees rooftops mountains
    silver-gray as far as necks can crane
        tinfoil blocking heat and air

aluminum sky lets not one ray of sun
    not one dot of blue into its space
        spreading its gargantuan chest
            from end to end of heaven
            hogging it close

aluminum sky—dry dry high and flat
    it popped up high today
        to warn us not to hope
            not to expect

HOW POEMS ARE BORN

while walking room to room, to tuck
bedsheets in around the edge, to
wash my cup in morning light of
sink

drop soiled laundry in the tub, wipe coffee
stains from tile, sweep lint from sofa cushions
crumpled flat, fill cubbies with his
books

fingers, hands, legs move like 'motons
clearing dust, while poems rush in like
fools, disembodied, spinning reels of
recollection

stringing phrases, weaving words he spoke,
parsing empty spaces of the life lived here, making
sense of him and me and death, the poems are
born

NAMED STAR

You were always a star, but now
the midnight-blue certificate in my hand—
from hundreds of starry-sky miles and
thousands of moon cycles between these friends
and us—dispels anyone's denial.

Where exactly you are parked among galaxies,
only telescopes from mountaintops,
genius eyes glued to lenses, can know.

But here's a start:
Coordinates RA: 3h30m34.50s, Dec+47°59'43.1"—
And further proof:
Registry #10099-7897-1210054, the Official Star Registry.

Always a star.

THE AFTERWARD

I move because I must,
else I'd stay shrouded in quilts when sun slants in.

I rise because I must,
else I'd press fetus knees more staunchly to my chest.

I walk because I must,
else lead would spread through rebel bones.

I speak because I must,
else dust would fill my mouth as his.

SLEEPLESS

i toss and turn on pillows wet
figments more fearsome than facts
doubts dug deep in spaces worried dark

i had three to live my life with me—
husband, daughter, son—
now cut to two

he was plucked untimely
in the broad of day
so i cling to children with daily dread
they, too,
will be spirited away

BEST DAY OF THE YEAR

*"Write it in your heart that every day
is the best day of the year."*
--Ralph Waldo Emerson

yes emerson yes except *that* one when his heart crashed and i couldn't make it throb again though i was down the hall waiting as his eyes went blank

and though i used to save him from the precipice time and again bedside wife-hawk when whitecoats erred or nurses flitted from his room too soon

and though my fingers drew a blessing on his forehead kissed his nose tweaked his chin and he said *i'll see you in an hour*

and though they wheeled him like a mummy down the hall we knew so well smiling and unafraid of tiny nicks they'd slit into his arm

and though you're always right emerson your brain transcending us i must disagree emerson for that *one* day that day that one day I couldn't save him

COME TO MY PATIO

...and see.
This is why I can't stay sad:
Mounds and mounds
of yellow blooms
bloating their ceramic
homes with bounty!

And these weeds,
delicate clover
with creamy petals
at their heads,
intermixing.

Poppies multiply
magically,
unabashedly uninvited
in this terra cotta bowl
brimming with begonia,
kalanchoe, and violet.

Like mixed-up crayons
in a child's box,
their colors bemuse,
bewitch, and promise
surprise.

FIRST GRANDCHILD

1.

Lizzie was lifted from her mother's womb,
umbilical cord wrapped around her neck, blue and in distress. *Miracle baby,* they said, *not a second too soon.*

And the featherweight package with fine blonde hair and
anxious lungs became the first of many things:
first of her generation for Papa and me,
first grandchild to cajole our middle-aged muscles and bones into
      climbing slides and trees, monkey bars and swings.

She turned back clocks for us while turning our faces
into her future as we, mostly Papa, cared for her since infancy.

2.

The graduation stage sits outdoors banked with potted lushness—
      white lilies, pale carnations, palm fronds with slender arms
      outstretched—
empty for now, awaiting 80 white-gowned
princesses to grace its planks and stroll across,
redolent arms filled with goose bumps and bouquets.

A bluer sky could not be found this June,
nor a more brilliant sun,
than what offertory gods display today.

3.

In identical chiffon dresses grazing high-heeled shoes,
Lizzie and her classmates walk single-file down the middle aisle
      to full-throated cheers.
She makes us proud, petite princess finishing Mayfield in style,
      embraced, photographed, encircled by kin.

This is the day these girls have waited for, their dream day...
      the day Papa waited for since Lizzie learned to talk.

4.

Radiant little girl who used to run Papa ragged each day he
        picked her up from daycare after work,
radiant little girl who made Papa slide down every slide, in
        every park, swing every swing,
made Papa carry her on brawny shoulders for ice cream in the
        snack shop down the street,
used him as make-up model in her teens,
sat beside him as he tutored her in trig,
planned their celebration of her high school graduation months
        away.
She made Papa proud.

5.

His seat is empty next to me on the Mayfield lawn,
and as cellphones flash and groups huddle for the lens,
I scan the sky, now puffed with clouds, and watch tall treetops
        shimmy in the breeze,
looking for a sign,
perhaps a cloud parting briefly for an extra burst of sun,
or a butterfly alighting on my hand.

He dreamed this day, and this is his.
With Lizzie, this is Papa's day.

III.
Mournings

THREE BOTTLES

of cologne—yours--brands
you liked: Rivers &
Towers, Antonio Banderas
Seduction in Black, and
Brut...yes, Brut...un-
ashamed, long-necked
bottle, poor country
mouse perched by
brass faucets, by marble
tiles on your side of the
sink, rubbing musky
shoulders with
the Macy's guys

and you splashed
them joyously on chin
and neck, then spread
their joy onto your
chest and arms, and...
yes, between
your legs

but Brut was always
best, your #1, elixir
from your high
school days, your college
nights beneath stars
on country roads,
you handsome guy
that smelled so good

oh, there were other
bottles of parfum sprays
endorsed by rock
star studs, and after-
shaves hawked
loud by rappers
and billionaire jocks--
bottles sitting on
your closet shelves

but Brut took you
through banquets and
weddings, wafted you
through humdrum days
and luminous nights,
you in tuxedo and
cummerbund, you
modest Texas boy,
morphing in gravitas
with passing years,
you and Brut
smelling so good

three bottles--Rivers,
Banderas, and
Brut--triplets
conjoined arm to
arm, standing
calm on my side of the
sink, manly bottles your
manly hands held,
holding your
place, evoking
your scent, your
face, in morning
hours and empty
nights... invoking
you

POTTY CAT

He greets me every morning
as he did you,
coiling himself into a fuzz of gray
at your feet,
green eyes mesmerizing you
to drop your pants
so he could crawl
into the crotch warmth,
burrowed in
for the duration
of your sitting.

BROKEN HEART SYNDROME

There is such a thing,
doctors say--not
the zigzag-split pointy hearts, two
pasted halves on Hallmark cards.
No, docs say, hearts really do fall apart.

Disasters shred our fibers like thieves picking
pockets in broad day. Suddenness of things gone wrong, small or big,
chip chunks of stamina and strength
from hearts like Greenland's glaciers sliding into
open sea. Our chambers are invaded, locks picked,
thresholds split, so heartbreak can slip in.

Yes, doctors say, there is such a thing.

A violent spat, a gun jabbed in your face. A lover in his mistress'
embrace, caught in your bed. A husband with a
bullet in his head, or found suddenly at dawn, blankets warm but skin
cold. Startling things, ambush-grief, unplanned loss, faith shattered and
tossed. World upended, though brief, can be enough to cleave your heart.

Yes, doctors say there is such a thing.

No wonder, then, that spouses married long and tight, depart this world
in tandem, or one soon after. No wonder, then, that when Carrie,
princess of galaxies, died sudden, her icon mother, consumed with grief,
followed close. No wonder, then, that elders in love for life die days
apace.

Yes, not all wounded depart, but they
stumble along, with fluttering hearts, weakened
pulse, leaking valves, raided chambers... puttering
onward, broken heart syndrome and all.

Yes, doctors say there is such a thing.

OUR HOUSE

    will never be
        the same again
                satan storm swirling
                    while spirits slept
            shredding roof
                      rending windows
                          blind
                tilting timbers
            dissolving walls
        to chalk
          and
                dust

FEBRUARY 3, 2019

Our wedding anniversary today, 51 years
if you were still here. Rain that stayed away
when we surrendered you to earth last fall
pummels me when I bring you a bouquet.

We celebrated last year's 50th with dinner and
champagne. Now I walk the grass alone, mist
hovering on headstones as I wend my way
to your ribbon of ground.

Companion tears clouds send soak my parka
black. My rubber boots sink in sod and
upturned soil on new plots. At your shoulders,
your marble pillow slick with rivulets,

I lay flowers like those you used to
give, like what you would've set on my bedstand
this morning if you were here. Bouquets
you gave for 50 years.

WHEN THE TIME COMES

"To live in this world
you must be able
to do three things:
to love what is mortal;
to hold it
against your bones knowing
your own life depends on it;
and when the time comes to let it go,
to let it go."
--Mary Oliver, "*In Blackwater Woods*"*

All our flailing, testing,
beseeching gods to shield our transience
end in dust.

Only one thing never dies, and
that is you clasped to my breast, and
me sewn into yours, both blind
to doom that always separates.

We've known since birth, since
our primal breath, that mortals' love
is marked, is clocked,
but still,
we
love.

---

*Oliver's poem originally published in her book, *American Primitive*, in 1983.

INSTEAD

1.

My husband and I didn't always
see eye to eye—or "I"
to "I"— and sometimes looked across
a divide with "you" and
"you" accusingly.

Marathon arguments
sometimes spilled into dawn
and beyond, wore us limp and
made us question if our
vows could bear such ire.

The issues didn't matter—children,
money, workloads...
or more petty: tennis, words in
songs, mundane events—   who said what, when,
where, why... silly, willy-nilly things
unworthy of recollection
or retelling.

2.

But there were stacked-up days when
instead of quarrels, we embraced
our children in our laps, spun them in
carousels, lifted them into
treehouses, rolled down grassy hills of museums,
took them to tidepools, rollercoasters, Lion
Country safaris. Days when we camped
beneath redwoods instead, curled in blankets and
bags near roiling Pacific waves.

Guilt keeps a brutal scorecard,
tally strokes broad and dark, overshadowing
points lined meekly underneath Rightness.

There were stacked-up days when we instead
walked on Maui sands, black and fine like
sugar. Stood on Grand Canyon rims instead,
admiring sunsets like tapestries woven by
tribes. Climbed Gem Hill in the inland
desert instead, and stuffed our pockets
with jasper. Leaned on Eiffel Tower fretwork
instead, admiring the eternal fishbowl
of Paris lights.

3.

Half-a-century of anything is washed in
tides, capstones churning white,
sands of shells by rocks shown clear when
waters slide far out. Ebbs and flows, highs
and lows, mark the decades of our lives
lived long and close.

Our hearts remember hurt more
clear than joy sometimes, but
half-a-century collects treasures and
detritus much the same, with
treasures often drowning the
pall of pain.

TABLE FOR ONE

Rather *queenly*, come to think.
Dressed in pearls and patent heels, I'm the
one! Waiters bow, starched towel on bent arm,
pull out the velvet chair. There's something rich
about sitting where I want, corner table near the
palm, merlot crystal, crooner glossing
grand piano keys, smiling at me.

Rather *queenly*, being one, *the one,* my wrists
gilded with bracelets he wrapped in silk
last spring and gave me with a kiss. So elegant, this
booth padded to the hilt, and mahogany table
sized for one, just one, not big enough
for him and me.

So *queenly* when the doorman at the Ritz
holds the stained-glass door, sweeps
his arm at chandeliers. Something rich in bow-tied
waiters murmuring French bottle names
they cradle in hands
sure and athletic like his.

So, so *queenly* to be alone, just one,
one and only, like on a throne knowing
you're alone up there. Royalty has always
been deemed thus: lonely job, they
say. Being top gun is exclusive:
queens, shooters, whatever, just the best.

First time I came here, he held my hand, unused
to fancy places, him and me. But it was our
first anniversary, and he wore his best blazer, black
leather loafers (shined!), and he walked me to this
corner nook, beaming at just *being there,*
just being, and ordered champagne.

CLOCKS

If I could turn back clocks, I would, to
squelch grievances that once seemed
grand, with tongue that slapped and teeth
that bit our souls in half.

If I could turn back clocks, I would, to
wrap my arms around your waist, and
lay my head beside your cheek, and
kiss your fingers, to hold firm and

press our flesh in peace, to say these
puny matters sunder us and foul
our home, unworthy of one breath, one
word, one inch of space,

just dusty air. I'd turn the clocks, then
face them down, then send them
to the alley bin, and say let's celebrate
the rays of sun awaking us today,

the meal we ate in candlelight last
night, the neighbor who brought
peaches from his tree at noon, our
grandchild at your piano yesterday.

Clocks measure hours and minutiae,
small in ticks and tocks that often trick,
but we swim in galaxies of memory, of a
million hours' worth of affirmations.

ORDINARY THINGS:
Tanka Sequence

"Do small things with great love."
--Mother Teresa

I.

WORK

His drugstore glasses
nestle in bamboo tray, lens
wiped: well-worn helper
to zero in and solve brain-
busting calculus problems.

Dog-eared books line up
like troops by gray gooseneck lamp—
Homer, Egypt, Rome,
Civil War—blue coffee mug
stands guard past midnight.

Cups and cups of pens,
all colors, sharpened pencils,
wisely picked, ready
for grading pupils' papers
stacked high in leather briefcase.

Bronze tennis trophy,
historic! --first championship
in 100 years:
his coaching crown, students proud,
collective, endless triumph.

2.
SELF

Behind the door: his
meds bag, flap loose, with crumpled
Kleenex, insulin
syringes capped in orange,
glucose pills at the ready.

His walker stands shy
by his desk, at his service;
brown folding cane holds vigil
by the door: his extra legs,
aluminum bodyguards.

Like a scientist,
he logs daily doses of
his medicines precisely,
arranges pills in colored rows
in labeled plastic boxes.

CDs, radio,
cassettes, stereo earphones:
for napping, reading,
family trips, and, mostly,
stirring memories he loved.

3.
FAMILY

He gave us nature
as a balm we'll always have:
cool shade, birds splashing
in gurgling fountains kept filled,
birdhouses on trees and stakes.

Nature showcased bright
in our spacious yard: twenty
fruit trees, beds bordered
with boulders spilling blooms, vines...
potted plants parked on patios.

Large redwood deck he
built with trellises and roof
overlooks gardens
he birthed through fifty years' toil,
planting ongoing glory.

Such ordinary
things he touched with fingers kind!
Such ordinary
things he did and gave for those
he cherished and left behind.

SOMETIMES

...we just need to
clear our heads, shake
them hard with eyes on clouds
and wisps that float to corners of heaven

eyes on golden slants that light up curled
edges of gingko tree leaves, tiny
spotlights teasing sparrows on high wires

sometimes we just need to
keep eyes up, above treetops, beyond
cumulus parked on mountains
as far as our heads can tilt

keep eyes soft when we lie on
grass, to see the infinite blue of
humanity's roof, the ocean birthed first

sometimes we just need to
elevate eyes to air, wind, ether,
weightless realm of eagles, lightness
and all that is good

OLD HABITS

How easy it is, how easy,
for the brain to trick us
into wiping pain away,
into thinking you're here at my door,
or in the kitchen by my side, sipping
at the mug, sighing at the early hour,
calling my name, your
mouth at my ear.
How easy, how easy.

The brain contorts memory
to shadows of itself, clipping
connections to calendars
and seasons, children growing
into future mists we veil over when
we're tricked. I hear footsteps,
jingling keys, the gentle click
of a door unlocked, water lapping
at your washbowl, gentle, curling,
steaming stream gurgling, and
you humming as you shave your neck.

How easy it is
to hear these precious sounds again,
these tiny tunes of love,
tricking death and me with
double shots of cruelty: warmth
at the reliving; then stabs
of recollection,
of seeing you lowered,
sinking,
roses sliding
to the soil.

DREAM #1

five weeks gone, you
step light in my dream, half
of you, your

profile clear, calm in
dusk, dark blue cap and
shoulders curved in

thought on the red bench you
built beneath the cottonwood
shading your deck, gazing

at the half-acre you tilled
decades past, fruit trees
heavy, moss layered on serpentine

boulders guarding garden
beds you molded with ungloved
hands when your hair was black

November 2018

DREAM #2

i'd stumbled days on end
seeking home
        through gulleys   lined with rocks
hills of burrs   open roads that called
    but lied
strangers shifting form,
        known then not
  threats to life
            freeways far below
and high nearby
    then melding into blurs of
                clouds

i don't know how
i came to you
           or where
 a house i never saw
     a room unwalled
          a bed i'd seen before
the night you died
  half a gurney now
             unmoored

sheet up to your neck   face smooth
  you gazed
at me without your glasses
smile sublime
understood
i crumpled close
   oh papa
      oh oh oh
syncopated breaths
         throat raw
  papa
    papa
       oh oh oh papa

December 2018

DREAM #3

another crazy-quilt of stopping points: airport gates, stadium seats,
doctors' waiting

rooms—i searched through each fleeting space
alone, hands bare, past open mouths,

souls on pause, people pinned between forced
patience and their wants, stolid

folks with canvas face unstroked, waiting for clocks' hands to nudge,
for ticks to tock, for

ticket-takers to boom out numbers, athletes to explode from tunnels,
whitecoats to hear our litanies. i

stumbled through a crowded clinic till l saw
you, in your best suit, in the middle of

the space, like center stage, glowing, set apart,
your face expectant as l wended my way to

your enfolding arms that pulled me to your perfumed
breast as mine trembled and heaved with grief.

January 2019

LIPS, LIPS

An anniversary dream,
that's what it was—
your gift to me after
being gone a year, after

being absent from
my dreams for months,
after forgetting me
up there in your airy

halls. I have no doubt
you came to me last night
with the gift of *you*
and only you, your lips, your

gentle mouth pressing mine,
your special gift,
to make up for time taken
from me in soul-breaking absent

dreams and absent arms,
being gone so long,
then you appear in one
extended scene with nothing

but your loving lips, full,
soft, exploring sweetly
my lips, my lips only,
with the slow attention you

used to give when we sat side
by side, or lay weary in darkness,
your lips brushing mine,
dreamy in life as in dreams.

October 5, 2019

IV.
Balms

SO MUCH GOODNESS IN THIS WORLD

I marvel at unconditioned love,
The givers giving when cameras are off,
Microphones stilled or gone,
Without name tags, the press,
Tax breaks or trophies,
Unpaid.

Like Pope Francis in Argentina,
Touring slums after work, alone,
Holding dying hands in shanties,
Walking in his orthopedic shoes
In debris and darkness, door to door,
Unsummoned.

Like my Grandma Guerra,
Cooking breakfast for my eight siblings
And me when Mom drove to work
100 miles each day to support us all.
Grandma cleaned, washed, babysat,
Unwavering.

Like my dearest Papa,
Tutoring math students at lunch,
Before and after school,
Placing family above himself,
Building and planting a homestead we love,
Unconditioned.

CLOUD GODS

cloud gods got together this morning
coated lapis on ceramic skies
swooshed cotton contrail on distant hills
and disappeared the streak in pines

got sun to slant on hopscotch puddles
holding fast to concrete cracks
mirrors shimmying my steps
sun coaxed from hiding just for me

who stationed birds on this burly arc of oak
this arm that bends close to my path
who posted birds on this fountain by the fence
bubbling invitations to swoop and bathe

who sprayed all these picket fences white
fixed gates and put geraniums by new posts
got garnet blooms to tap me as I pass
recalling I'm the widow down the street

rain and record colds have prisoned me
with books, keyboards, calendars, clocks
but cloud gods popped genie lamps today
to make this magical world my gift

TREMBLING LEAF

A trembling leaf on my orange tree
tells me there's a village scout
in the branch, a faithful worker
in a velour suit seeking sweetness
for his queen and comrades
back at the hive.

So I await with breath abated, bending,
peering at the aromatic tremor,
waiting for the blur and buzz of
the seeker to appear.

He emerges smiling, triumphant,
but not before shaking things some more.
Suit pristine, shoes dusty with his work,
he shows off dance moves
on the airy floor, then butts his hips
on a few more leaves and weaves away.

No, he's not drunk with nectar,
just an emissary as we all are,
from queen or gods, joyful in due
diligence, in doing for others.

BALMS

*"When we pivot ... to the blade of grass, the note
of music, the line of a novel, ... we breathe
and are revived."*
--Ava Du Vernay

Each place I sit, and take a breath
to catch a break from life,
simple gifts from earth, ocean, sky,
from gods and goddesses of all that is not man,
suffuse me with their balm.

On my patio, on tables under gingko trees,
in backyard bowers of jasmine and pine,
in cottage rooms darkened with dusk
or lit by morning sun,
gifts I've gathered soothe my grateful eyes:

>Stones rounded smooth like eggs, roosting
>serene in bowls and nests fashioned by hand.

>Rocks shaped like hearts, adopted from creek
>beds, forests, deserts when I take our dog around.

>Shells iridescent, fragile, crescent, large like
>helmets, or conches furled unto themselves.

>Bamboo platters piled with sand and bits of
>wood the waves spat up.

>Pine cones nestled in orange rinds, their
>fragrance intertwined.

>Petals sprinkled across tablecloths with
>beeswax candles and pedestals of pears.

I waft from room through room,
from garden to patio and back,
bits of nature greeting me at every turn,
to calm, to keep me grounded to the dust,
to sands, wind and sun, trees and rocks,

to keep me grounded
to the mighty and the small,
to all that we've been and will be again—
to keep me grounded to
the simple and the simply grand.

BONSAI

1.

cuts are gentle, kind
a nick from blade,
snip from shears,
bending of limbs in nuanced arcs,
baby branches coaxed
with copper twined
on base and slender arms

moss mounds ranged
like eggs beneath the bonsai's
infant shade--
velvet ground for mist,
for spray from
long-throated sprinklers,
my magic wands i wave
at shoots and tender leaves

2.

these bonsai plants were yours,
and mine, learned together with
museum trips, garden books,
jaunts to palm springs
nurseries and huntington

you bought these glazed
and decorated dishes
we filled with junipers--
redolent bushes, scratchy, curvy,
living treasures we could
shape and mold

you placed this terra cotta temple
in this bowl, by this Chinese
fisherman, and this pagoda by the rock,
three ceramic scholars in its shade--
bringing life to life

3.

early morning sun
brings peace,
a swirl of simple joy at
gentle arcs of limbs,
velour floor beneath
our ficus, maple,
and baby pines

this peace is yours,
and mine, in waking day
or dusk as I walk
among our bonsai
and feel your spirit
in their leaves and loam

4.

the future waits
on each bonsai we birthed,
each princeling
replete with promise
for ages hence—

beyond you, beyond me,
decades more,
when our children's children
tend to gnarled trunks,
burly arms,
leaves filled with centuries
of air and cloud,
roots pushing toward gods

LOVELY THINGS

1

There are no monopolies, no corporate takeovers, conglomerates, or elitists where lovely is concerned.
Money, titles, heritage, accolades, top dogs pulling strings to beat one out over the other.

Nuh-oh.
Nope.
Nothing like that is even a breath whispered in the same mouth uttering the word "lovely."

2

No billionaires, sheiks, crown princes in concrete lines of succession. No Nobels, Pulitzers, Oscars, Emmys, Grammys, Tonys, Speakers of the House, Majority Leaders, VP's, or any of these nonsense designations of something meriting admiration.

Nuh-oh.
Nope.
Not at all.

3

Titles and labels don't pass the test of time, the test of smell, sight, taste, and truth. Lovely is not a decree, a petition signed by millions, Executive Action pummeled down throats (sometimes) by narcissists. Not a legal writ, Constitutional Amendment, or multi-national treaty.

4

Where power is entrenched, enshrined, enabled, and ennobled, authenticity dies. Lovely dies. Where decrees spread far and wide, ensnaring millions into nets of acquiescence and consent, with or without freedom, with or without victory dances, parades, cathedral bells pealing long into the night, cavalcades of limousines like black beetles choking streets, brass bands trumpeting into the helpless wind... lovely dies.

5

Lovely is beyond decree.

Lovely is omnipotent in its invincibility, its mercurial soul ungraspable, undefinable, unchainable, indefatigable, and indescribable...though poets try.

6

Like this—
    Lovely is small: a pearlescent nodule on an ocean shell.
    Lovely is global: a super moon omnipresent
        simultaneous over landmarks cast across continents.
    Lovely is soft: the smallest toes of the first grandchild.
    Lovely is hard: ombre-streaked red cliffs in deserts
        decorated by eons of elements.
    Lovely is uncontainable: coils of galaxies pin-pricked
        with heavenly behemoths.

7

And this:
    Lovely is like water: indispensable.
    Like sunbeams: clockwork regimentation of presentation
        immune to whim.
    Like air: lifting, uplifting, filling, not filling, seeable and
        unseeable, refreshing, chilling, and killing.

8

Lovely is below our feet on mossed forest floors, above our heads in red-dawn morning runs, beside our legs with angel-children in strollers, on our chests with infants dozing, in our laps with beribboned Shih-Tzus napping.

9

Poets try to pin down lovely.
We try
we try
oh boy do we try.

STONE HEARTS

I collect them every chance I get:
under shrubs dried from winds
that sap life out of things, or in
gurgling streams. Stone hearts
buried beneath others like them,
stones misshapen by elements.

Stooped by creeks
like a miner seeking gold,
I scan gray, white, brown, beige, black
stones arrayed like faces in a crowd.
Smooth rocks that glint in sand,
or craggy stones lying with clods
and scorpions
and dung beetles
in thorns.

A heart's a heart.

Doesn't matter where it hides
or shows itself,
how wind and sun and storms
have buffeted or cosseted,
how it's been tossed
or laid in moss.

I gather these stones
in pockets by my breast.

BIRDS, BUTTERFLIES, AND BEES

eternal beauties of this world,
the three B's...
birds, butterflies, and bees

evanescent balm in whirrs and hums,
swoops and dips, lighting and leaving,
flitting, fluttering in arcs no plane can make

no other flight machines or
flights of fancy penned immortal
match a fleet of birds, butterflies, and bees

no snip of poetry
no sip of bacchanalian sweetness
surpasses the passes of their wings

V.
Resolutions

40 DAYS OF WANDERING

> *"It is believed that the soul of the departed remains wandering on Earth for 40 days after death, coming back home, visiting places the departed has lived in, as well as their fresh grave, before leaving for the afterlife.**

October 5 to November 14: your 40 days.
Tell me, Papa. Did you really go abroad or stay close to where your life played out?

> Did your spirit float a thousand-miles-plus to roots entrenched but blurred with time: your all-boys' boarding school by Rio Grande, where you broke rules but cupped chalices in the chapel for priests to fill with wine?

> Did your spirit float to your mother's humble grave, now obscured with Texas vines, beseeching her to wait for your embrace at your next home?

> Did your spirit float to Henrietta Street, newlywed house, walls unsheathed and poor, where we brought our firstborn home and dreamt of smoother paths?

40 days, Papa, 40 days of viewing and reviewing in your disembodied state.

> Did your spirit stroll in our Pasadena garden, sit by Buddha in our corner nook, amidst his temples and rounded stepping stones at his meditating feet?

> Did your spirit remember with the Perfect One the gold and orange koi once gliding in the pond beneath the bonsai pine as you snoozed on our concrete bench?

> Did your spirit rest on the deck you crafted weeks on end, when you hammered redwood railings keeping children safe, handrailed steps, trellised roof-- a sheltered cove where we sat and laughed, broke bread with friends, kin and neighbors, or just sat alone in evening dusk, just the two of us?

40 days, Papa, before leaving earth forever, before walking head held high into the afterlife.

> Did your spirit pause beside our bed, look down on me in troubled sleep, then gaze upon our son working midnight hours to secure his daughter's college dreams?

> Did your spirit pass by grassy high school fields and dusty chalkboards, where you'd coached and taught and uplifted generations?

> Did your spirit circle back to your final bit of land, the one you saw as it was dug, the one you saw before it filled, the one mounded with moist loam and roses, the blanketed one with marble stone, the one you glimpsed from high in clouds as you broke the bonds at last.

---

*From a brief article about Catholic doctrine on the internet, author unknown.

CANDLE

*Death is not the end of the light;
it is putting out the candle
because the dawn has come.*
  --Tagore

    aurora's
    fingers
    pinch
    flame
    spread
    iridescent
    skirts
    on
    clouds
    fan
    gray
    away
    dawn
    can't
    die
    light
    never
    snuffed
    galaxies
    prove
    this

365 DAYS

ago
this very day,
ides of october--
heaven's loan
expired
and we rendered you
back
to the pulling arms
of earth,
stood
on the brink
of the maw
that takes
back
love on loan:

        its chiseled space
        boxed air
        boundless void
        with false bottom
        still, like stone--
        our loan was called
        and we rendered you
        back
        to greed-gods
        who hoard
        immortality
        for themselves,
        who take
        back
        breaths on loan--

we circled the maw
as inch by inch
you sank
in its throat,
settling bravely
on rocks and loam,
you not crying,
knowing your loan
was called,
your home now dust,
knowing we
rendered you
back
to all that was, is,
and shall forever be.

PIECING THE BREAKAGE

There comes the day when we resign
ourselves—as Hindi brides stepping into
the pyre—to the impermeable.

The cudgel of loss has struck, and it
will not unswing itself.

We grind teeth, gird tired loins,
and plod on—blind, limping, bleeding,
broken, or miraculously soothed—
into the new *what is*.

Piecing the breakage together again
may take priests, imams, wizards,
shamans, or crystal ball gazers...
elders, lovers, books, pilgrimages...
or whatever trods the journey of loss
with us.

But the journey has been walked.

All roads face forward from here.

---

*Originally appeared in a prior version as "Acceptance" in the author's book, *Reading Tea Leaves After Trump*.

ALL OUR EXPLORING

"The end of all our exploring will be to arrive where we started, and know the place for the first time."
--T. S. Eliot

Beginnings are endings, endings are beginnings.
Who can know the difference, and
what's the point of knowing?*

The Egyptian sphinx asked passersby:
"What walks on four legs in the morning, two at noon, and three at night?"

Although the old man with the cane is not crawling,
he's closer than the other two to dust, of which he came.

Obsolescence walks side-by-side with us each path
we tread
until the end.

OAK BEHIND THE DENTIST'S OFFICE, LAKE AVENUE

Never saw you, full frontal, till today,
when I wandered weary from the coffee spot,
eyes bleary from books and screens, to this parking
lot buckled and leaf-strewn.

The sun is high, half-hidden in clouds airbrushed
like smoke, but sunburst filaments flash here and there,
a cliché photo of forest tree
leaning into center where we blink.

Your knotted arms and swooping legs circle back
unto themselves, curlicues high and low,
creating cradles for human birds,
teasing us to break bonds with earth,

To coax ancient legs up toward sky,
to hug bark and branch and inch our way
through leaf and scratch and tanglements
to reminisce on what we are:

Travelers in middle spheres: children, men,,
elders, midwives, hugging earth, bound to roots
yet brushing brows with stars and satellites,
mortals mixed with god and heaven dust.

LET THERE BE LIGHT

> *"Why do people keep asking to see /*
> *God's identity papers / when the darkness opening into morning /*
> *is more than enough?"*
> —Mary Oliver*

I flood my rooms each daybreak--
slide drapes, lift shades, swing doors to
do the god thing: bring in light.

Outside, the moon's a faded coin
on trees and clouds, an old woman with
her luster stripped who knows and waits.

Inside, the sink streaks gold, rays swathe
stone floors, the cat blinks and slinks down
from the tabletop, sun-blind.

My calendar can't tell me how my day
will go, lauded or denuded, how far my
psyche slips, or if I shine.

But at dawn, my hands are wands
that banish blackness, for it's true: what they
say, about god inside, god in each of us, how

we're
all
god.

---

*"I Wake Close to Morning," in *Felicity*.

AFTER THE LAST ACT

No curtain call for me.
When the drama's done, soon or late,
I'll rush backstage
and seek you out.

You'll be there.
Our tears will be our "Bravo!"s
as we meld our soul-bodies
into one again

and smile at the scenes I botched,
my anemic lines of heroism,
my maudlin moments,
my final soliloquy of hope.

You played the script before
and left the boards not long ago
to sit backstage and wait for me.
You knew we'd meet once more.

And so we shall.
I'll set up residence backstage,
immortal lovers, you and I,
after the final act.

DEAREST PAPA

Husband.
  Father
    Grandfather.
      Teacher.
        Coach.

Like a string of precious pearls, royal pearls, your life was this.

We might add "Son" for the mother who abandoned you when you were two but did so with a sundered heart. Without conditions, *your* forgiving heart found her decades gone, and healed hers.

We might add "Brother" for three half-brothers and half-sister your father gave. Though miles and circumstances cleaved your paths, you later won their love.

We might add "Neighbor" for our fellows up and down our street, from backgrounds vast, small, dark, light, folks who'd greet you, and you them, every morning, every day for years.

In any storm or brilliant day, in dusty village or world-class town, in leafy road or busy street, your humanity shone like a lamp in destitute alleys, like a comet in swirls of stars. Shone unforgettable.

Afterword:
FROM A STUDENT

[Excerpted from a former student's letter received soon after Papa's death]

Dear Thelma,

    I was saddened to hear of Vic's sudden passing and wanted to pass something along that I have thought about over the years. When I look back, sometimes I think about pivotal moments in my life, strange little crossroads, blips really, where events that may have seemed inconsequential at the time turned out to have life-changing impacts. One of those involved Vic, and I wanted to share it with you.

    You may not recall that when I was attending Santa Monica City College right after high school, I was struggling in the last math class I ever took, Algebra II/Trigonometry, not exactly rocket science but for me it might as well have been. I was working that class hard and studying a lot, but I never had an aptitude for mathematics. Your husband knew I was struggling, and he tutored me. . . a lot! He never asked for a thing in return, and I strongly suspect he would have much preferred to be playing tennis. He showed me extraordinary patience and generosity of time and spirit. In the end, and surely due to his tutelage, I passed that class with a C-. It was probably the most effort I ever put into any class for such a mediocre grade, but I was proud of it at the time.

    That unimpressive C- changed my life. UC Santa Cruz had granted me "conditional admission" if I passed that course. I would not have been admitted and would probably not have gone to college if I'd failed. While at UC Santa Cruz, I interned at the Legal Aid Society and learned to love law. In turn, that internship drew me to law school and eventually to my present legal career. The grade I received in that piddly junior college math class had a ripple effect on my life that I could not have foreseen, and I couldn't have pulled it off without Vic's help.

I've thought of that grade over the years as one of those pivotal events that changed things for me. I don't think I ever properly thanked Vic (I still think of him as Mr. Reyna) or ever told him that those weekends he spent helping me instead of watching his beloved football games made a difference beyond what he knew. I just wanted you to know what I will always remember Vic for. I offer my sincere condolences to your entire family.

 Sincerely,
 Jordan

ACKNOWLEDGMENTS

FOR PRIOR PUBLICATIONS:

The following poems were first published in a prior version as shown below; some appear in this book with significant revision.

- "Spoons": *Breath & Bone* (Finishing Line Press, 2011).
- "Convalescent Hospital": *Lummox Anthology #8,* 2019.
- "This Is How Grief Goes": Published as "Depression" in *Reading Tea Leaves After Trump* (Golden Foothills Press, 2018).
- "How Poems Are Born": *Spectrum Anthology #19,* 2019.
- "Stone Hearts": *Free Love 2 Anthology,* February 2014.
- "Old Habits": *San Gabriel Valley Poets' Quarterly,* Spring 2013.
- "Balms": Published as "Talismans," *Poetry & Cookies Anthology of Poems,* 2013.
- "Bonsai": *San Gabriel Valley Poets Quarterly #66,* Spring 2015.
- "Piecing the Breakage": Published as "Acceptance" in *Reading Tea Leaves After Trump* (Golden Foothills Press, 2018).
- "Sometimes": *Reading Tea Leaves After Trump* (Golden Foothills Press, 2018).
- "Let There Be Light": *Rising, Falling, All of Us* (Golden Foothills Press, 2014).
- "After the Last Act": Published as "After the Final Act," *Breath & Bone* (Finishing Line Press, 2011).

FOR WONDERFUL PEOPLE IN MY LIFE:

I hold closest to my bosom the little family Papa and I created, whom he cherished more than anything or anyone on earth, and who have been the bedrock of our existence: our son Victor Cass, daughter Christine Reyna, and our three grandchildren—Lizzie Cass; and Charlie and Cassie Reyna-Demes. I also cherish Lizzie's mother, Jeanette Dickson Valdez; and Charlie's and Cassie's father, Charles Demes.

My gratitude for the kind, loving, supportive people in our lives overflows to our extended family, fellow poets and other friends, colleagues past and present, clients, students, neighbors. Good people are the globe's most precious gems, the greatest treasures. I'm thankful they share their paths with us.

ABOUT VICTOR A. REYNA, JR.
1944-2018

Photo by Thelma T. Reyna, 2018

Victor was a first-generation American, the son of a Mexican immigrant. Because of extreme poverty, his father had never attended school, but he served in the U.S. Army in World War II and earned American citizenship. Victor's mother, born in a nondescript, impoverished Texas town, likewise had no formal education. Victor's mother walked away from her marriage and her son when he was two years old, and he never saw her again till his high school years. His father raised him alone, with a portion of Victor's childhood spent in a Catholic boarding school more than a hundred miles from home.

But despite their meager roots, both of Victor's parents at different times in their lives opened small businesses—the father a barber shop; the mother a religious/mystical shop in her garage selling candles, rosaries, perfumes, knick-knacks, and homemade food to go. (She called that part of her business "Chicken A-Go-Go"). Both were hard workers with loyal customers and earned enough money to make ends meet. Each parent remarried not long after their breakup and had other children. Thus Victor had four half-siblings, all of whom he later got to know and love.

From these humble roots, Victor defied the odds. He had been identified as a mentally-gifted student in his teens. For his high school years, his father sent him to San Antonio to live with relatives. Here Victor was a voracious reader and a talented athlete. His participation in sports teams throughout his high school career helped instill discipline, self-esteem, and deep confidence in him.

Victor always imagined himself as a success. His father, a disciplinarian who nonetheless doted on him, expected that Victor would earn a degree, something relatively rare for poor Latinos in the early 1960s. Victor became the first graduate in his family, earning a high school teaching degree with majors in math and chemistry. His path in life was clear. He became a vaunted high school math teacher for 36 years and a championship athletic coach.

∞

I met Victor in his senior year at Texas A&I University (now Texas A&M) in Kingsville, Texas, my hometown. The qualities that attracted me to him were the ones I cherished most: a quick wit and ineffable sense of humor; a childlike willingness to play... ping-pong, chess, skateboarding, all of which we did on our "dates" in between classes on campus and which later endeared him famously to our three grandchildren.

Other traits: His natural intelligence, inquisitiveness, and inherent skills in everything that interested him: carpentry, landscaping, camping, coaching, backgammon, piano, baseball, football, tennis, history, science, math. His thoughtfulness and protectiveness toward our family. His perseverance.

His life, except for his illnesses, was how he had envisioned it: a tight-knit family like he'd not known before marriage; a vibrant professional career; a life diametric to the poverty and loneliness he'd experienced in his Texas beginnings. He traveled across the ocean, across the nation, helped open the world to our children, grandchildren and me.

As he often said, "I'm always where I want to be." Indeed, and this gave him joy.

50th Wedding Anniversary, 2018
Sushi of Naples Restaurant, Pasadena
Photo taken by our favorite server

ABOUT THE AUTHOR

Photo by Victor Cass, 2019

Thelma T. Reyna's books have collectively won 14 national literary awards. She has written 5 books: a short story collection, *The Heavens Weep for Us and Other Stories;* 2 poetry chapbooks—*Breath & Bone* and *Hearts in Common;* and 2 full-length poetry collections—*Rising, Falling, All of Us* and *Reading Tea Leaves After Trump,* which won 6 national book honors in 2018. As Poet Laureate in Altadena, 2014-2016, she edited the *Altadena Poetry Review Anthology* in 2015 and 2016.

Thelma's fiction, poetry, and nonfiction have appeared in literary journals, anthologies, textbooks, blogs, and regional media for over 25 years. She was a Pushcart Prize Nominee in Poetry in 2017. She received her Ph.D. from UCLA.

National Award-Winning Literary Book Press:
Over 100 authors published in Southern California

Our indie-published books have earned over 20 national book honors. Visit our website to see our poetry collections, war novel, and a memoir, at www.GoldenFoothillsPress.com .

Author **Thelma T. Reyna** is available for literary events, book signings, classroom presentations in high school and college, book clubs, panel presentations, and as a guest speaker or workshop presenter on varied topics.

Contact her at:
www.GoldenFoothillsPress.com
goldenfoothillspress@yahoo.com

PAGE FOR NOTES

PAGE FOR NOTES

www.ingramcontent.com/pod-product-compliance
Lightning Source LLC
Chambersburg PA
CBHW021955290426
44108CB00012B/1077